BUILDING BLOCKS OF FINANCE

CAREERS IN FINANCE

Written by Lauren Kelliher

Illustrated by Graham Ross and
David Kurtz Williams

WORLD BOOK

a Scott Fetzer company
Chicago

World Book, Inc.
180 North LaSalle Street
Suite 900
Chicago, Illinois 60601
USA

For information about other World Book publications, visit our website at www.worldbook.com or call 1-800-WORLDBK (967-5325).
For information about sales to schools and libraries, call 1-800-975-3250 (United States), or 1-800-837-5365 (Canada).

© 2022 World Book, Inc. All rights reserved. This volume may not be reproduced in whole or in part in any form without prior written permission from the publisher.

WORLD BOOK and the GLOBE DEVICE are registered trademarks or trademarks of World Book, Inc.

Library of Congress Cataloging-in-Publication Data for this volume has been applied for.
Building Blocks of Finance
ISBN: 978-0-7166-3975-6 (set, hc.)

Careers in Finance
ISBN: 978-0-7166-3983-1 (hc.)

Also available as:
ISBN: 978-0-7166-3991-6 (e-book)

Printed in India by Thomson Press (India) Limited, Uttar Pradesh, India
1st printing March 2022

WORLD BOOK STAFF
Executive Committee
President: Geoff Broderick
Vice President, Editorial: Tom Evans
Vice President, Finance: Donald D. Keller
Vice President, Marketing: Jean Lin
Vice President, International: Eddy Kisman
Vice President, Technology: Jason Dole
Vice President, Customer Success: Jade Lewandowski
Director, Human Resources: Bev Ecker

Editorial
Manager, New Content: Jeff De La Rosa
Associate Manager, New Product: Nicholas Kilzer
Sr. Editor: Shawn Brennan
Sr. Content Creator: Lauren Kelliher
Content Creator: Jenna Neely
Proofreader: Nathalie Strassheim

Graphics and Design
Sr. Visual Communications Designer: Melanie Bender
Coordinator, Design Development: Brenda Tropinski
Sr. Web Designer/Digital Media Developer: Matt Carrington

Acknowledgments:
Writer: Lauren Kelliher
Illustrators: Graham Ross and David Kurtz Williams/The Bright Agency
Series Advisor: Joel Chrisler

TABLE OF CONTENTS

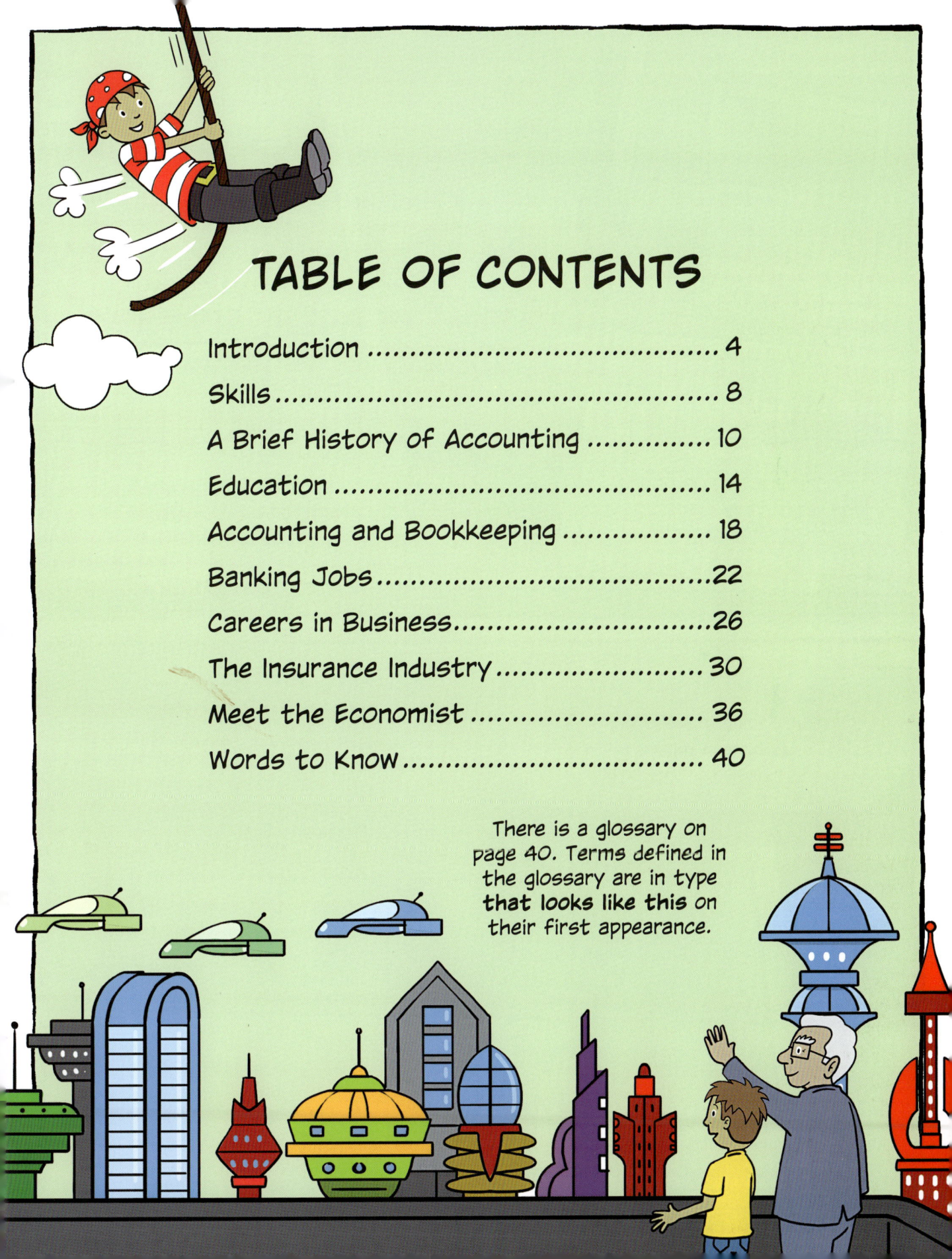

Introduction 4
Skills 8
A Brief History of Accounting 10
Education 14
Accounting and Bookkeeping 18
Banking Jobs 22
Careers in Business 26
The Insurance Industry 30
Meet the Economist 36
Words to Know 40

There is a glossary on page 40. Terms defined in the glossary are in type **that looks like this** on their first appearance.

INTRODUCTION

People are always asking kids what they want to be when they grow up.

Some of my friends want to be rock stars or astronauts.

But I have a different future in mind.

Hi! My name is Bo...

...and I want to be just like my uncle, Mr. Banker.

Uncle B. is never short on cash...

And, he's able to help other people take care of their money and build their own wealth.

"I'm already on my way."

"In school, I love math."

"I love to be the banker in my favorite board games."

KING OF THE CASTLE
PRESS START

I love playing video games that let you build things and gather wealth.

Look, I built this simple farming village...

...into a bustling castle town!

Someday, I'd like to have a finance job in real life.

Let's find out how I can get there.

SKILLS

I'll need many skills to work in finance.

Math will be an important skill...

But, it's far from the only one.

Hard skills are things you can learn in school...

...like knowing a foreign language or computer programming.

Soft skills are important, too.

Soft skills are also called people skills.

They include listening, teamwork, communication, and *etiquette* (manners).

Some jobs in finance require managers, problem-solvers, and innovative thinkers.

Etiquette COACH

Soft skills can be just as important as hard skills in these jobs.

THIS WAY TO HISTORY →

A BRIEF HISTORY OF ACCOUNTING

Whoa, Uncle B! What are you doing here?

I thought I'd get you started... at the beginning!

Probably the first dedicated finance workers were **bookkeepers**.

But, that doesn't mean that they collected books, like a librarian.

Bookkeepers, both then and today, record financial *transactions* (dealings)...

...keeping a record for a business or other employer.

"Follow me!"

"Accounting and bookkeeping date back to some of the earliest known civilizations."

Detailed records of transactions have been found in the 5,300-year-old tomb of King Scorpion I in Egypt.

To Ancient Egypt

11

There were also bags of tokens made of bone or stone...

...with numerical symbols on them.

They were basically ancient receipts...

...and *inventories* (lists of goods and materials).

Skilled people called scribes did many of the accounting tasks.

Scribes took inventory of the pharaoh's goods and taxes...

...often writing on papyrus and bone or clay tablets.

Who wants to bring these taxes to the pharaoh?

Sounds like a job for me!

EDUCATION

What kind of education do I need for a job in finance?

We sure could use someone who's great with numbers.

In high school, I'm going to take as many math classes as I can.

Some schools offer a course in personal finance.

I could learn to make a budget...

...pay bills...

...and save for major purchases.

It may also help to take economics, communication, and computer classes.

Some schools will have a business, investment, or finance club.

I even decided to run for *treasurer* of student council.

A treasurer is a person who manages a group's finances.

Once I graduate high school, I want to attend college.

LANDLUBBER UNIVERSITY
HOME OF THE KRAKENS

I can pursue a degree in finance or accounting.

It will take about four years to get my bachelor's degree.

That will qualify me for an office job at a bank or financial firm.

FINANCE 101

If I want to continue my education...

I can apply to earn a master's degree in finance.

This will open job opportunities in investment management, risk management, and trading.

If I want to go one step further, I can get a doctorate degree in finance.

This will enable me to become a researcher or financial instructor.

ACCOUNTING AND BOOKKEEPING

Let's imagine I graduate with a bachelor's degree.

I'll need a job.

I need a bookkeeper for my accounting firm.

POOF!

What luck!

Welcome to the company!

FOREST FINANCIAL

18

Modern bookkeepers are not so different from their ancient counterparts.
They record all the transactions a business makes.
They also organize and classify each transaction
We keep it on the "books."
The company will use this information to make business decisions.
The information I record is important to people outside the business, too.
That includes the business's bank, its investors, and the government.
CLUNK

Panel 1:
Whoa, this stuff looks pretty complicated!

How do businesses make sense of all this data?

Panel 2:
That's an **accountant**'s job.

Accountants analyze and interpret financial data.

Panel 3:
Accountants may use the data to create reports...

REVENUE

...and give advice based on those reports.

Panel 4:
But that's not all we do.

Accountants are professionals who help people to manage their finances.

20

Accountants help businesses big and small to take care of their money.

Many accountants work for the government.

WOODLAND REVENUE SERVICE

They collect taxes and help government agencies manage their finances.

Some accountants even help families and individuals.

A FAIRY PUBLIC Accountant

Many people seek an accountant's help when preparing their taxes.

BANKING JOBS
Actually, I've always wondered what it would be like to work in a bank!
POOF!
Off you go, then!
1850
BANK
That's more like it!
Howdy, partner! Come on in!

Customer representatives, like Miss Daisy here...

...are the first people you see when you enter the bank.

We're great at answering questions

We can help you to deposit or withdraw money...

...and provide other basic services.

We may even help you open a checking, savings, or retirement account.

Customer representative is a great job for someone who likes working with the public.

You don't even have to have a college degree to get started.

23

WANTED: MONEY FOR COLLEGE

Customer representatives aren't the only people who work at the bank.

Ol' Pete here is our bank's **loan officer**.

Er... that's right!

When it comes to loans, I'm the sheriff of these parts.

LOAN OFFICER

Loan officers work at banks or other institutions that lend money.

CLIK CLIK CLIK

Panel 1: I help people borrow money...

Panel 2: ...to pursue higher education...

Panel 3: ...start or expand a small business...

HECTORS HATS — OPENING SOON

Panel 4: ...or even purchase a vehicle or home.

Panel 5: But first, I have to make sure you're a good credit risk.

FLIP FLIP FLIP

Panel 6: Otherwise, it's happy trails, partner!

WANTED — BAD CREDIT

CAREERS IN BUSINESS

There's no telling how far you can go with a career in finance.

Every large business employs finance professionals.

Near the very top of most major companies...

...is someone called the CFO.

I'm the CFO, the **chief financial officer.**
I'm the highest official in charge of my company's finances.

It's my job to make sure the company is doing well financially...
...paying the necessary taxes, and following its budget.

But I can't do it alone! In addition to accountants and bookkeepers...
I rely on a number of specialists... I'll show you some!

"Whee!"

"Let's go!"

Budget analysts organize and secure funding for a business and its activities.

They create a spending budget based on the company's revenue.

Credit risk analysts assign credit scores and credit ratings.

They decide how *reliable* (or risky) people and institutions are as borrowers.

"Whee!"

"Careful now!"

"Hurry up now! Time is money!"

Financial analysts provide investment advice...

...help companies expand, and predict performance based on industry data.

Statisticians analyze data.

They make reports that help companies and other organizations to accomplish their goals.

I'm right behind you.

Market research analysts study how products sell.

They divide customers into different *demographics* (groups) by age, income, and other traits!

Wait for me!

Right this way!

Huff! Huff!

Investment bankers help corporations trade on the stock market...

...and acquire or merge with other companies.

Up here!

Which way?

THE INSURANCE INDUSTRY

"Look out!"

"Are you okay?"

"Luckily, I have **insurance**."

WHAM!

"Squawk! Hello! I'm this hamster's **insurance agent**."

"Insurance is a service that protects people against risk."

30

Each month, this hamster makes regular insurance payments.

In case of an accident or other disaster...

The insurance company may help pay for the unexpected cost.

Many financial professionals work in the insurance industry.

As an insurance agent, for example, I help people figure out what kind of insurance they need.

Homeowners insurance can help to repair damage caused by fires, storms, or other disasters.

Automobile insurance can help cover the cost of an accident.

AMBULANCE

Health insurance can provide money for medical treatment.

And that's just a few of the many kinds of insurance.

Insurance agents are not the only professionals who work in the insurance business.

JUNGLE INSURANCE CO.

Risk managers calculate the financial risk of making insurance investments.

THREATS
• TIGER
• ANACONDA
• CROCODILE

An **actuary** is a person who gathers all kinds of statistics.

These statistics are gathered into tables that predict the likelihood of insurance claims.

Insurance and other financial decisions are so complicated.
It seems like there should be a job just helping people make good decisions.
There is!
We're called **financial planners.**
OPEN 24 Hours
CLICK
I can help you to budget your money, plan your insurance...
...pay off debt, and develop an investment strategy.
OPEN 24 Hours

My job is to help you meet your goals...
Whether you want to buy a home...
SOLD
FOR SALE
...start your own business...
BO'S FROZEN BANANAS
...travel the world...
...or even prepare for retirement.
CONGRATULATIONS BO!
I'm a little young for retirement.
You're never too young to think about building wealth.
Before you retire, though...
I'd like to introduce you to one more financial professional.

MEET THE ECONOMIST

I brought you here to meet my friend.

Hi! I am an **economist**.

An economist is a scholar who studies business activity on a large scale. Hop in!

I study the relationship between society's resources...

...and the goods (and services) people produce.

I study labor...

...to determine if there will be enough workers to get the job done...

36

...and supplies to see if there will be enough material available.

OUT OF STOCK

Economists often put their findings into presentations...

...for academic researchers, companies, and government offices.

I've seen a lot of jobs today, but I think I might want to become an economist, too.

What made you decide on that?

Because this guy is almost as interested in finances as I am!

37

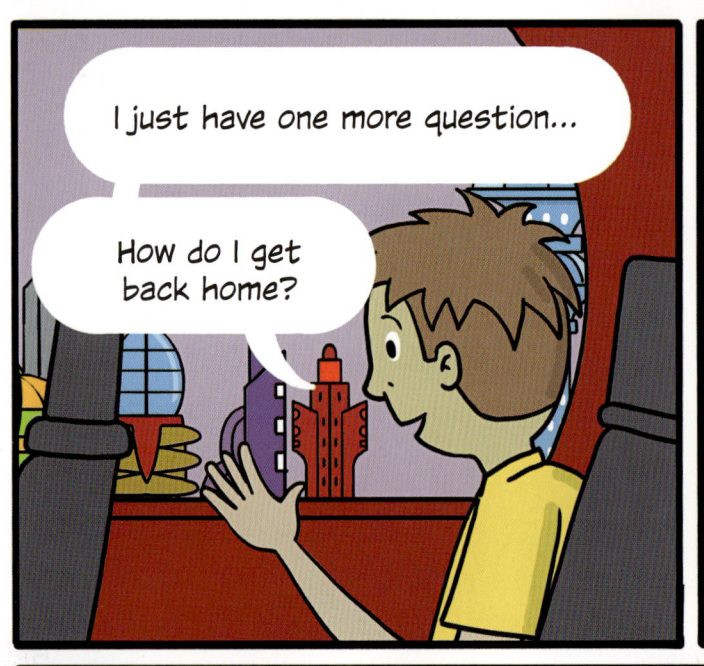

I just have one more question...

How do I get back home?

I can take you there...

Buckle up, you two!

I think I see a shortcut.

Just remember this, Bo.

Whether you choose a career in business...

BOOM

ZAP

...or in banking...

...or in accounting...

A good education is the key to a successful career.

And, even if you decide not to choose a financial career...

Knowing about finance can help you in any career you choose!

WORDS TO KNOW

accountant a person whose job is to keep, inspect, and analyze financial accounts.

actuary a person who compiles and analyzes statistics and uses them to calculate risks.

bookkeeper a person whose job is to keep records of the financial affairs of a business.

budget analyst a person who helps businesses organize and allocate their financial resources by developing a budget.

chief financial officer a senior executive with responsibility for the financial affairs of a company.

credit risk analyst a person who reviews and assesses the financial history of a person or company to determine if they are a good candidate for a loan.

financial analyst a person whose job is to assess the financial condition of a business to determine if it is a sound investment.

financial planner a person employed to manage the personal finances of clients.

insurance a means of providing protection against financial loss.

insurance agent a person employed to sell and manage insurance policies.

investment banker an individual who often works as part of a financial institution and is primarily concerned with raising money for corporations, governments, or other entities.

loan officer a representative of a bank, credit union, or other financial institution who assists borrowers in the loan application process.

market research analyst a person who studies and analyzes data on consumers to help companies understand what products people want, who will buy them, and at what price.

risk manager a person who takes responsibility for identifying, controlling, and reducing the financial risks a business faces.

statistician a person who mathematically analyzes data to answer specific questions or solve problems in business.